MW00561615

Praise for *You, Always Near*

The love poems in *You, Always Near* limn the tender mysteries of a lover's death, even as they explore the "confluence of hearts." Pamela Warren Williams brings us love at the hospice bed, love in the days after the surrender. "I try not to reach for you," she writes, and yet each poem is a tribute to the ways love helps us reach beyond the self into the beauty of communion with another. Each poem "reassembles the magic" of giving ourselves to another. Each poem brings us an unanswered question, a gift.

— Rosemerry Wahtola Trommer, author of *Hush* and *Naked for Tea*

Warren Williams takes us on a bittersweet journey in this collection of poems. First, there is the joy of a love shared, so connected that she finishes his sentences, that he goes down on bended knee when she takes a fall. Yet too soon, we are brought to a more profound intimacy, as her husband slips away from life, leaving her behind. These poems are not only about a lost love, but also about finding that love is unceasing, persistent, continuous.

— Elise Stuart, author of *Another Door Calls*

During that resurrection of loving memories we share in divine moments, that is to say eternal and deathless moments that lovers experience poetically as the poet "sorts through the refuse of all that is left behind."(*Clues*) Along with the lessons and dreams that are lost the gift of laughter abides. Williams is a highly skilled imagist: in *Collecting Communion* she begins with the lovers "following Geronimo's tracks, while certain that he left none" and ends by comparing bats freefalling from their "water tower" nest to the Perseid meteor shower. These beautiful juxtapositions reveal the heart of Warren Williams' collection. Even though remembering cannot retrieve the ecstasy of the original, poetry is the closest we can get: the lover is gone, within the rhythms of verse lies the consolation of understanding.

— Goyo, Professor Emeritus, UNM, author of *Shallow Rooted Heart*

Pamela Warren Williams captures the visceral nature of grief as if it were the elusive blue morpho butterfly in a temporary net. These poems are iridescent, poignantly accurate portrayals of resonant loss. Yet, they also contain lightning strikes of hope that even grief at this depth of opaque blue can be transmuted to radiance. These beautifully crafted poems, dedicated to a husband now gone, transcend the personal and aim towards a comprehension and resolution of loss at an ecumenical level of compassion.

— Eve West Bessier, Poet Laureate of *Silver City and Grant County*

In *You, Always Near*, Pamela Warren Williams offers us a glimpse into the life and work of her late husband: poet, mystic and spiritual warrior Stewart S. Warren. Continuing the rich legacy of Mercury HeartLink publishing, she speaks lovingly about the beauty and grief found in this life. Through her eyes of gratitude, Pamela, like Stewart, invites us to journey into the great mystery beyond the veil.

— Mary Elizabeth Van Pelt, author of *In Silence I Speak*

Pamela Warren Williams's poems are a collection of heartfelt and tender remembrances of her late husband Stewart Warren. These beautifully crafted poems are intertwined with her devotion and deep sense of loss with the humanity that Stewart brought to all he wrote and to all those he touched.

— Mark Fleisher, author of *Reflections: Soundings from the Deep*

Mercury HeartLink
www.heartlink.com

You, Always Near

the Stewart Poems

You, Always Near
the Stewart Poems

poems by pamela warren williams

heartlink.com

You, Always Near – the Stewart Poems
Copyright ©2021 pamela warren williams

ISBN 978-1-949652-07-9
Publisher Mercury HeartLink
Silver City, New Mexico
Printed in the United States of America

Front Cover image: *Scripted Destiny* painting by Alexandra Eldridge
www.alexandraeldridge.com
Photo on back cover by Belynda Webb
Photo with author bio by Katney Bair
Photo of author with Heka by Lisa Kirksey

All rights reserved. This book, or sections of this book may not be reproduced
or transmitted in any form without permission from the author, except for brief
quotations embodied in articles, reviews, or used for scholarly purposes.

Permission is granted to educators to create copies of individual poems,
with proper credits, for classroom or workshop assignments.

Mercury HeartLink:
consult@heartlink.com

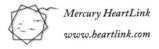

Mercury HeartLink
www.heartlink.com

To be in love opens all
possibility, narrows the path,
calls forth a singular beam.
— Stewart S. Warren

Preface

This is a love story, and I am not beginning at the beginning. That part was scattered throughout my first book, *Hair on Fire*, http://amzn.to/2eD5lxL like confetti or puzzle pieces of dreams from another incarnation. The inception of this book started after we devoured the gifts of Italy and during the phase that Stewart referred to as our mutual need to go off and finish growing up. In my naivete, there was a time when I would have argued about my own need for that. Ultimately, he was right, of course. My sadness now is that we were both such late bloomers, although in sync as always. We spent the intervening time circling around our collective center, becoming and burnishing who we were to be together.

This collection of poems represents my version of that path without a roadmap, replete with the breathtaking truths of our newfound deepening: of joy, of shared mysticism, of lessons, of co-creation. Then despite our living every day by stubborn determination, firmly in gratitude for each moment, Stewart's cancer announced the upper hand. Without warning we were thrust into the liminal space of a month in hospice. Since Stewart's transition, rich in humility for both of us, and the ultimate honor for me,

I have spent the last year reassembling myself, relearning self-sufficiency, finding new ways to serve and to grow, and talking to Stewart every step of the way. Suddenly, it made perfect sense to me to continue Mercury Heartlink, Stewart's publishing business of twenty-six years. So, this book of my poems honoring our shared path is your introduction to this new chapter. Thank you for joining me on the journey.

—pamela warren williams

Acknowledgements

Just as with my first book of poems, *Hair on Fire*, I have been led each step of the way by all the right people. Sheila Seclearr, my editing angel, asks all the hard questions and makes me a better writer. Denise Weaver Ross handles details as they beg to be handled, and at warp speed. Both appeared on my radar at exactly the chosen moment. Even the plan for selling the heartlink domain was fated to languish until it was my time to rebirth the business, suddenly recognizing that open door. As always, my chosen family in California has had my back in finding my way through the maze of a new endeavor, with Kim Webb inevitably rising to the occasion. The warm tight community of Silver City has been ongoing comfort and support, from before I was even a resident here, cheering me on as a visiting poet, and offering endless resources and connections. Julia Robinson is a champion in the warm art of connection, and Dale Ruklos is the ultimate charming host to us all. I have never felt so welcomed anywhere in the world. I am humbled and grateful to my dear reviewers and to John Roche for the glowing introduction. The way that I have been carried along on this mysterious leg of my life journey has been nothing short of miraculous, revealing a wondrous faith in my path, from my first moment of synergy with Stewart, through our shared passages and unreasonable joy, to this exhilarating new precipice. And I continue to feel Stewart's guidance as I take this leap, with so much gratitude for it all.

Contents

Up Country

Planetary Rotations

Goodbye from Here

You, Always Near

To Stewart, of course, with all love and infinite gratitude for first seeing me as a poet and for supporting me so grandly, always. And to all of my poetry friends and family who have supported my path with such love and encouragement. And so, here we are, birthing the new incarnation of Mercury Heartlink!

Introduction

It is my pleasure, indeed, to acknowledge the rebirth of Mercury
HeartLink Press, and an equal pleasure to introduce its first publication,
this exquisite book by Pamela Warren Williams. *You, Always Near: the
Stewart Poems* celebrates the life of Pamela's late husband Stewart
S. Warren, a superb Southwestern poet and the founder of Mercury
HeartLink. This book recounts the couple's circuitous path to love as well
as their joint pilgrimage on a Rosicrucian or "Episcopagan" path wide
enough to encompass Buddhist and Native American spiritualities. It
chronicles Stewart's last months and Pamela's resilience in the aftermath.
This is also a book about one writer's journey to find a voice equal to the
task of telling this story.

A sense of place exerts powerful influence in the "Up Country" first
section (and throughout the book), particularly their home in Silver
City, adjacent to the magical Gila Mountains of southwest New Mexico,
with trips to the Gila Cliff Dwellings, Cooke's Peak, and Lizard Head Pass,
or Sabino Canyon in Arizona. These poems extoll the "smell of spring
emerging in the canyon" and the visual delights of "Mountain mahogany,
desert varnish, the expanded family of artemisia."

Especially charming are the poems in the second section, "Planetary
Rotations," addressing the aptly named Heka, "Guardian dog of our web
of love." Each day's journey for Pamela and Stewart included walking the
dog, or, more precisely, walking with Heka through Gila wilderness.

The third section, "Goodbye from Here," concerns Stewart's final journey,
and Pamela's role of caretaker and guide to "navigating hospice."
Selling his car, "remembering your joy unfurled at the wheel, on each

spontaneous drive." Noticing, "My hand sticky with morphine, my mind equally sticky with conflicting emotions." Regretting that "I had not yet learned your topography."

The fourth and longest section, "You, Always Near," concerns Pamela's coping with "this new silence, deafening," in the months following Stewart's death. While searching for her "own true north," she circumvents roadblock after roadblock to "the reassembly of [her] being." Even "One Week Accomplished" is cause for celebration. Yet soon she must confront a new kind of isolation as the pandemic arrives in her small town, friends now masked, even as she tries to part the veil separating her from the beloved. In a dream, she finds, "Somehow, unknowingly, I had slipped through the veil, gravitating instinctively to your side, searching out that glowing smile."

I hope you will enjoy *You, Always Near: the Stewart Poems*. It is a courageous book that confronts the doubt, confusion, and pain of losing a loved one to cancer. A book that celebrates the small joys of encountering, and surviving, each day. And a book that quietly offers us tokens picked up on the author's journey, tokens that might very well prove essential.

John Roche, Placitas, New Mexico
Co-Editor of *Feeling the Distance: Poems by Stewart S. Warren* and
Offerings for the Journey: Poems for Stewart S. Warren
(Poetry Playhouse Publications, 2019 and 2020)

You, Always Near
the Stewart Poems

poems by pamela warren williams

Up Country

Buzzing Tranquilly

Chipmunk hilarity over the mislaid moon.
Shared love of wisdom acquired,
with its ensuing epiphanies.
And now, we are both blessed
by those sweet trusting eyes,
knowing, leaning into life and its travails.
What an inestimable and timely gift,
this gentle teacher.

Reveling in words,
alternate interpretations triumphing.
Plenitude of tales,
until silence insists.
Never enough time or
just exactly enough time.
Ever enough time
to marvel over
all this artistry and grace,
to gather her images.
Distilled naturally by
the prescribed glow.
Emerging truths
in this prayer bowl.

Dropping into comfort.
Shrugging off the outmoded chainmail
of the unabashed heart.
Discovering new ley lines.
Following foreign threads,
ancestral and precognitive.
A payday for the mosquitos
joining that sojourn in the woods.
Unacknowledged in the
sublime suspension
of the moment.

Clues

I read what you wrote about Benabbio again,
probing for clues on this path, as memories
of our Italy trip faded.
The word trajectory appears for
the second time on this definitive day.
and still less clear in this context, with so much unsaid.
Such sorrow that further examination
would be required
to even recall the divination of it all.
Our vision subjective as always.
I sort through the refuse of all that is left behind,
cataloging regrets for the loss
of lessons and dreams,
and most of all, the reverberations of the laughter.

Determined Warrior

Sometimes, now, I know to be still
just as instructed while a young rebel.
As in, keep your multitude of opinions
to yourself.
Rather than "No squirming in your seat."
I let you have your plate of vagaries.
You had that answer in last week's visit.
Different scene on the game board, now.
Do I trust you now, more deeply,
knowing how to forge my own way?
To raise my vibration
with a myriad of new tools?
When I think I know some tendency.
Some sorcery of overcoming evidence.
A path to assert some knight within.

Celebrating Heka

Sometimes cancer therapy appears a drum kit,
electric bass and high-end amp included.
In this case, a lovely, lanky dog
with a dazzling and continuous grin,
dispensing magic and medicine,
as is his legacy.
The warp and weft of your frustrated fury
tangled with self-pity,
make this a more likely conclusion
than perhaps imagined.
New habits will be required,
flexibility tested.
Moniker of the Egyptian god,
he appears knowing and serene.
Trusting. Leaning into
life's next venture.
This meeting of two grand hearts,
for deliberation
upon whom the rescuer may be.

Still Stringing Necklaces

Back alley entry
to Episcopaganism.
She laughed.
Similarities noted
to the deep darkness
of the Cosmic Campground,
and to the delight
in its unexpected gifts.
Pearls to be strung
on the necklace of understanding
that is this odyssey.
Limitless in potential
for how many glorious pendants
to adorn and illuminate the way.
The tells of this transit
reverently passed
hand to hand, as in any such
game of illusion.
Elevated communion
in the mosh pit
of this pilgrimage.
Divine therapy.

Collecting Communion

Following Geronimo's tracks,
while certain that he left none.
Master of subterfuge,
sleight of hand and cunning.
Soldiers' coats on the soap yucca.
More than a worthy obstacle
to having all this land.

Tales of Billy and Elfego
lace these hills together.
Soothed by herbal remedies,
buoyed by that ever-present
current of words channeled.
Viewed through that internal
rosy cellophane filter.
That sideways wolf glance,
assurance of love and guardianship,
despite regional cautions
for anything resembling a wolf.

There were hundreds of those bats.
Did they queue up to freefall from their
water tower condo? Reclusive javelinas.
Sequestered Perseids, as well.
This entire dense time a planetary
offering, with fear transmuted to awe,
just as water to wine.

And what if I never find out why?
The questions demanding to
just be lived.

Mountain Climbing

Within reach, even at this majestic
height. Hearts coyly touching anew.
Reaching at once for our center.
So acutely aware of these
expanded miles between us,
and further adorned by
that infamous familiarity.
Deepening sweetness.
Long-distance seduction.
Annealing the vow.
Fresh willingness to subdue
colliding fears in this cosmic version
of Mother-may-I.
Hierophant beckoning.
Divining the way.

Hero of my Heart

Noticing newfound serenity.
Possibly the reckoning of that
cherished internal churning.
Smiling as my joy trails from
your fingertips. Reminder
of the reveals of your lessons.
Rampant synergy affirms.
Shared reading, writing, merriment.
Continuing to plumb new depths,
to test my strengths, as you
demonstrate your own tenacity.
Embracing the required discipline
for captaining this venture.
Repeating that there is but this moment
of boundless love and faith.

Planetary Rotations

This Work

In the world with you.
Distributing joy.
Cherishing this bliss.
This confluence of hearts.
Researching ways to spread relief.
Slowing down still more.
Remembering to breathe.
Time for new lessons.
Recognition, now, of wild mustard
and of beaver-chew.
And which way north
to knowing.
Trust in the proximity
of the intuitive explorer dog,
and of the bounty of
your golden glowing heart.
And of the perfection
of just those two red tulips.

Knowing

Uncanny, that from thirty yards
up the hill,
My presence at the window
is sensed behind you
despite your focus on
unseen beings beyond.
Now snuggled contentedly
in the latest snow,
wolf-paws tucked in.
No less alert to potential
interlopers to your kingdom.

Affirmation comes,
trumping your intentions
for that treed feral cat,
as you acknowledge both of us
disapproving from our cozy sofa, inside,
turning to challenge our gaze.

Rekindled

Toes browned by the desert sun.
Wisps of unfamiliar long hair
glued to my perspiring cheek.
Loyal love-dog at my heels, curious
at my meandering morning pilgrimage
through the rustic garden
on the edge of wildness.
Unfathomable, sometimes, still.
this reimagined life.
Reinvented, rekindled passion.
Affirmations tumbling over each other,
so often in beloved laughter.

Possible connections abound.
Creatives in this rocky Shambala.
Will you become a treasured friend?
We've all made some kind of leap
to arrive at this fiesta of a life.
Okay, perhaps my own more impulsive
than some.

Reflective in this oppressive muggy time.
I settle into the deeper dissection
of who I may be in this new costume.
Stacks of clouds of every style and shade
decorate the stillness.
Will any of them be ours?
Gossip consists of who got a downpour
and what air-cooled sanctuary serves.

Plain Weird, Deliciously So

Ooh, critter alert. Presumptive visual
for a deer in the road. Or I suppose it
could have been an elk. Arising, dead center
on that two-lane, stock-still, a specter in
the black night of rural New Mexico.
But we neither one saw a deer, in fact.
First sighting appeared as an oversized Airedale
calmly straddling the center line as he viewed
our approach, eye-to-eye, head to one side
and in black and white as though a projected
hologram. Slowing way down, we watched
what had become a deer of the same size
and in normal technicolor sauntering off the tarmac.
"Wow, I could have sworn that was a giant dog."
"I know, an Airedale."
"Yeah, absolutely an Airedale."
"And it was in black and white."
"Before it became a deer."
"A deer in the color of a deer."
Loving the magic, we dissolved into
our customary shared giggles.

Don't you just love all the mysteries in
a New Mexico night?

Local Dialect

Discourse so often exchanged
in our private dialect
and peppered with assorted enigmas.
Smiling as I finish your thought
and then with great delight.
Your quick mind races through
our lives, like the express train.
I leap aboard,
eager for new plans,
the next adventure.
You have brought the soundtrack
designed for this moment, sublime.
And then you speak in tongues
to the dog, replete with
exaggerated hand gestures.
We are both certain
that you speak to us
of love.

Gila Alchemy

You walk out of sight.
I practice solitude
in the lea of your protection still.
Deep listening to
the wind's conversation with
the trees high overhead.
Studying the honeyed texture
of those mountain pines.

I smile at your reappearance
bearing a bouquet of soft feathers.
Bounty of some prior incident
with sacrifices.
Purification.
I announce my own sojourn.
Testing the healing of my
newly frail feet,
as well as the strength
of the dog's bond.
He stays ever closer to me.
Guardian dog
of our web of love.

Unalome as a Tattoo

Under a moon surely full,
one final healing
at the conjunction
of an open chakra chalice
and an overflowing heart.
Preparations, deep in the embrace
of the Saguaros of Sabino Canyon.
This latest fool's path
strewn with both Spring blossoms
and their accompanying thorns.
The sternum leads in procession,
surer now of power held,
of certainty earned.
The Church Ink priestess, Marcella,
here to dialogue with
my stubborn insistence,
simplifying this journey
still more in disallowing time.
My warrior claims my focus,
gifts me with the larger questions,
Tools for this initiation.

Conjury and Gratitude

Yesterday's riches began with a four-dog Sunday at the New Church of the Southwest Desert. Blessings to Reverend Carla for creating such a warm and welcoming Oasis. Moringa in the drinks, no less. Much darlingness among the canines, though one of them talked through most of the service. The visiting pianist shared her glorious creativity and the food of fellowship was most definitely divine. The man, the dog, and I then ventured off into our neighborhood to the Gila Cliff Dwellings. The Gila Wilderness, at over half a million acres, offers endless magnificence, inspiration, and humility. Around each hairpin turn, there is more grandeur, with endless vistas punctuated by more of those corrugated cliffs that I love so much. The cliff dwellings themselves tell many tales and elicit still more riddles from their inhabitants of the past. It was invigorating to see and smell spring emerging in the canyon, with my accrual of new identifiers. Mountain mahogany, desert varnish, the expanded family of artemisia. Then there was a cataloging opportunity for the dog to explore a bit of the river, with some lovely and ethereal white crane, floating off overhead. That leftover clam and mushroom fettuccine with salad from the bounty of the neighbors' garden could not have been a better welcome home. A candle-lit bath of my favorite West Marin Trees, quenched by the last glass of crisp cool rose and including pillars illuminating the shadows of the outrageous spring irises through the French doors, topped off a day of wonder over how to express so much awareness of grace.

Goodbye from Here

The Definition of Okay

You never fail to ask if I'm okay,
hearing a foreign noise from
another room. You still do, from
that hospice lair. Who will know
if I am okay or not? Okay.
A state I cannot perceive from here.
Anne says that the definition of okay
changes. The sadness and some
resentment debate today. Wonder over
Anita Moorjani's near-death miracle.
Why not your own? You, who would do
so much more good in this broken and
fearful world. Have I been praying
the wrong prayer? Too early, this
surrender? I have to practice more
trust. Thy will be done.

Writing the Journey

These frail threads of words,
ephemeral, elusive, and then gone.
Abandoned again to the warring factions
on my internal battlefield.
Imagining broadswords cutting
through the challenge to stay present.
To keep every fiber in touch with
this sacred time. This writing today's
meditation, and its glorious
sunrise on my face, another offering.

Savoring our last pipe ceremony.
Prayers in my heart and yours.
Still and always aware.
Mitakuye Oyasin.
The love and tributes continue to
pour over us. A deluge embraced
and savored in deep humility.

I resist the urge to stroke your hair
every single time I pass, or to
lament that none of those luxurious
locks were saved from your likely
last haircut, lovingly brought to
your bed. Another handkerchief,
I define, tempting another longing
for our myriad of shared smiles
and secrets.

Holding Time at Bay

We have rolled up the shade screens
dimming your view, inviting traveling Sol to
show us a new vantage on this twisting
path. Barging through Georgia's clouds,
disregarding unwashed windows.
Reminding, reassuring me of comforting
continuity, after your warm hand
no longer squeezes my own. You
promise that things will settle down.
The water will clear. I try not to see
that as potentially ominous.

It seems that the beloved dog lies
closer these days. Don't let me read
into that. Is that lies or lays? Please,
no panic that soon you won't be here
to remind me. I sigh, knowing that it
is already time to dust off my sword
and shield. I have already cut my hair
short again. Such a bittersweet
familiarity. That clear knowing what
works and what works so superbly.

Sentiment Required

Watching the flowers fade, a painful
accessory to this larger process. But
then I am told that there are no degrees
of magnitude. I cannot embrace that
one. Particularly not now. I see new
blooms on our hill. Thinking that I
must water and spend nurturing
time there, I try not to attach any
meaning to that suddenly snuffed
vigil candle.

I have kept my pendant on, a touch
of sacred geometry. Reminder
to hold fast to my heart chakra. My
still unfamiliar wedding ring a paradoxical
weight on my finger. Forged from youth
and fierceness. Reserved all those years for
this unimagined and inconceivable destiny.

Navigating Hospice

"I was going back to reclaim Scotland," you said.
"Were you, now?" "Aye."
Would this be our last shared laugh?
I had brought out the blade with the brass and
fruitwood handle from your altar. The endless
treasure hunt for more of your stories.
Did you tell me of its past? I can't recall.
And now there will be time. Unending time
stretching towards some hazy horizon.
Time for immersion in all your writing.
Our dear disciplined Phillip read *Flight Feathers*
cover to cover, so delighted in your shared bond.
Some of your history just too sad to absorb.
I have subscribed to your theory that too much
sentiment detracts from being in the moment.

You said that you are taking flight today, in fact.
You've leaned into the process of letting go of
your car, enough to smile at my packing snacks
and water for the tow truck driver from Albuquerque.
One of the perfect pears gifted for our union.
A couple of Julia's ginger cookies.
Surrendering the helm,
with tasks accomplished, and
some peace at last.

Such a tumultuous voyage, this life journey of yours.
Surely more than your allotment of challenges.
So many lives so courageously conquered.
And then the mentoring. Blessings
strewn to so many along your path.

The pinnacle of it all? This precious, sacred year.
Plotting our shared course, with gratitude
and awe for each day. Humbled by this gift,
this legacy of intentions to fulfill,
awareness and kindness to spread,
my own summit beckoning, as I wrap you in such
boundless love for your journey.

Sorrowful Practicality

Reclaiming your car. I won't mention
my angst to you over this version
of finality. And I promise myself
sternly, no regrets for that money
spent, remembering your joy
unfurled at the wheel, on each
spontaneous drive. It was all
utterly perfect, I insist.
My new mantra.

As I sob on the steps, watching our
happy travels towed up the Market
Street Hill, the dog follows the fence,
confused over this foreign departure
of his favorite transport to adventure.

Tender Inventory

I study you intently. Taking inventory
just as you would. And then reporting
in that way that so charmed me. I
stroke those wondrous unruly eyebrows.
Grandpa Henderson's, you told me.
I keep watch for another chance to
fall into the depths of my beloved's
blue eyes, now so erratically focused.
At times through the veil and in
holy moments on my tear-stained
face. I notice anew, that now-growing
freckle on the soft sun-loving ear
that I stroke so often. Irony.

Remedies

I stare dispassionately at the spider
over the bedroom door.
Medium sized, of indeterminate breed,
arguable threat.
Was it only two weeks ago
or maybe three
that I teetered precariously
over your hospice bed,
bare toes clutching the back
of the sofa, to remove its cousin
before it dropped on you?

Reminiscent of your stories of
scorpions losing their grip
on the ceiling.
Such wondrous hysteria we shared,
reading some prescription
for a piece of Plexiglas
larger than the bed
and suspended overhead.
Visions of us trapped beneath,
too weak with laughter
to extricate ourselves.

So, as I danced on the mountainous
ridge of the sofa back,
you offered, through your
veil of pain
that I might switch the fan's
direction for winter, as long as
I was at that height, anyway.

Helping You to Die

Searching for meaning in every move
and gesture. And for new offerings in
nurturing. A cool cloth on your forehead?
Another beverage from the expanded
menu? Are you hot or cold? Those pain
numbers became irrelevant somewhere
along the way. And then another query
from the nether regions of your journey.
My inner knowing works to translate
this new jargon, to collaborate in whatever
way I can in your search for the cosmic
portal. And then, ever the gentleman that
your mother raised, you apologize that
it's so much work for me.

Marking Time

Banished to the sunny far slope.
Good for both of us, you say.
I ask if it's too hard to leave me,
and promise again to be okay.
Unhappy, but *okay*.
I can still see your movements
through the open door.

I know too well how much
more you intended,
how much you've already
proved and I feel you dropping
your canoe in the river.
The light shifts
all too soon.
Now, I no longer sigh at each
motion of your feet under
my grandmother's worn quilt.
Is this long enough?
Enough wind beneath
those wings?
Enough prayers of gratitude
and for your peace?
Enough time
or beyond time?

Seasonal Sustenance

Everyone brings chocolate and I
obligingly eat it. Trying to remember to
get to that apple pie. Julia's understanding
of comfort food is my go-to. Transcendent
baked beans, mac and cheese delight,
and that mysterious toasted sesame
mixture straight from the jar. Meanwhile,
I try to keep pace with your weight loss
but in an upward arc. Pizza agrees
with me more than ever. Occasionally
I surface briefly in the real world, gasping
in befuddlement over the turning
color of the pear tree. How is that
possible? The sheared vinca reminds me
too, that fall looms. I work to not project
the potential challenges of this year's seasons.

Custodial versus Sacred

My hand sticky with morphine. My
mind equally sticky with conflicting
colliding emotions. Drenched in
sadness and love. Wondering
randomly why I cannot manage any
stretching or even those couple of dangling
return phone calls. Tomorrow, I will
insist on receiving housecleaning help as
promised. Debris of this madness
abounds. The battlefield for this life.
Worn out over the phone debate.
I was not trying to stop you from that
call – only the two others misdialed instead
of the intended ones. Your silence
into their voicemails was deafening.

Ready or Not

You ask me to come and sit with you.
Perhaps the final shared dawn.
Yet another piece of closure.
Many candles.
Sacred sage incense.
Native flute music.
You ask how to know
when you are ready.
I respond that your
work is completed.
Lists all checked off.
Difficult phone calls made.
A life documented in poetry.
You have loved me so exquisitely.
Spread encouragement
and instilled confidence.
Always new plans,
the promise of events.
Ever the provocateur.
Next is just to lean into it.
Surrender any perceived control.
The ultimate work, no?

The Labyrinthine Soul

Your smile today is blissful, full
of peace, as though some answers
were revealed. Stepping forward
from behind the ancient trees of
this dark forest. Can we write our way
to safety, do you suppose? To some
version of serenity, at least?

I continue to consider the constellations
on your bare torso, describing the
surface, the tangled terrain of
this soul. Still so dense in puzzles
to unwrap, to ponder, to be
divulged one poem at a time. How
long can that study contribute to comfort?
Succor to my endless tears.

Time Transits

The mid-afternoon silence on our
hill is deafening today. My spoon
mindful against Grandmother's worn
soup bowl. The same one from that
poem of our beginning. Now full of
our friends' healing nourishment. I ask
if you envision some celestial
restaurant as your destination, given
the endless clatter of dishes by
your side. Then, sated momentarily,
I write again, happy for your humble
vision of that flatbed truck approaching.
I inquired if it was a ford, while having
imagined something of far more grandeur
like an elaborate gilt chariot of the
Tarot. But I recognize the utter perfection.
My wise renegade coyote warrior.

Here and Everywhere

You tell me that there is a little more
time. I ask, what shall we do, then?
Infinite choices now in this nether realm
Once more over Lizard Head Pass?
A sunset shared on the bench at the
top of Boston Hill, capturing the
glory view of your 'wee willage'.
Or shall we make love one more time?
That roguish grin and twinkle in your
eyes vouch for your selection.
And then I thought later of that
proposed sojourn on the tropical
beach, languishing in your cherished
sunshine, sipping fruit drinks, laughing
in delight, and writing our way
intentionally into the cosmos.

Wishes Coming True

I always longed for a Soleri bell. For
overlapping tribal rugs of assorted
peoples, the perfect black travel pants.
A home brimming with meaningful art
and provocative books, surrounded
by inspiration. I did not know to ask
for the laughter, for being so cherished,
so much in tune every precious day.
So dense the studies, the unfolding
shared journey. Always new riches
to be revealed. So luminous, this time,
such an abundance of love. We've
left it strewn around town. And then
after all, when I can breathe again,
I trust that it will be the love that remains.
That empowers me to move forward
into the next unknown, writing my way
through it as you taught me.

Freefall Passage

Even sitting in the warm fall sun feels
frivolous today. You loved it so, out here
in our paradise, always trying to conquer
that endlessly invading inner chill.
Helping you navigate downstream through
this odyssey without signposts. Your
internal compass, always so certain, now
seeming to spin wildly. Can you access
divine guidance while in freefall?
I tenderly observe those fleeting dreams
of our toes in foreign sands.

Thinking of friends, wondering of their
daily trials. The continuum of time
still theirs. Such vivid truth of others'
hidden tales. Hold your beloveds
close, lest they slip away, unseen.

Faith

You call my name this morning,
say, Honey, help me?
I bend your knee tenderly
over a pillow.
Then over your shoulder, you ask me
if I know where to find...
I finish your question,
"You? Of course I will.
I never doubted that."
Is our belief driven by desire?
A need for some elusive certainty?
Faith born of this void?
When I cannot begin to envision myself.
Solo traveler in this paradise
co-created.

I trust the heat of this early sun,
piercing the treetops
to comfort and heal
my imploded center.
Some cathartic travel?
Meditative time
on our enchanted hill?
Creating adventures
with the buddy-dog,
who still brings your smile
when he comes in to
lick your hand.

World Without End

I had not finished learning your
topography. Memorizing those
constellations that pull me deep
into your internal cosmos. Now,
today, a specter of your former self
has appeared at my side. Pain-drenched
eyes. Labored breath. Beseeching
hands. You have loved this life and
me so gloriously. May this be your
day of grace. I imagine your whispered
okay of acquiescence. Surrender of
the bold venture of this incarnation.
I try not to reach for you. Not
wanting to impede your passage.
Depart with the knowing that you
are held so very dear, for always.

You, Always Near

Solo Now

This new silence, deafening. Sadly,
I know that there will come a day
without all these loud, keening,
howling demands. Will an answer
have come? No real expectation
of ever knowing. Cancer's assorted
gifts: humility, vulnerability, a more
open heart. All apparently with an
expiration date, a determined grip
on the preciousness of each sacred
day notwithstanding. An intermittent
headache. Result of such shouted
protest. Messages from beyond
the veil so often mentioned. Is there
a password for access? A single
month in hospice, while testing
patience for release from agonies. Now
hardly adequate to buffer this shock.

Time as a Construct

I have started wearing your watch,
disregarding time standing still. Or
perhaps more accurately, careening
past me. Blowback of the fast freight
passing me by. I am lighting the
candles despite the sun on my face.
Thinking that I want a warmer afghan.
Inviting the dog in at night. Imagining
the deep internal chill of the
impending winter. Struggling to
replace your gaunt departing
grimace with the radiant eyes
and laughing smile I so treasured.

Sustenance

Unprepared for this ascension.
Novice adept with wet wings.
You have left me a strong tribe who
seem to intuit when to lift me up,
to light my way. You speak to me
through our sister medium. My
sorrow too deafening to hear your
sure voice. Reassurance that you
are here for me. Guidance to continue.
The respite of your pain consolation
for the limitless void left by the
absence of your warm hand in mine,
your delicious laughter woven
with my own, your endless plans for
the next venture or event. Your
poems in my ear as they emerged.
You have left enough of those to
sustain me for a good amount of time.

One Week Accomplished

Eve acknowledged me for getting
through this first week. From in here,
it simply went by. Flowed on through
me. Did my howling outrage carry
me forward, I wonder? My passion
for deep connection; answering so
many warm and loving letters, so
much heart in evidence. And writing
through my pain and sorrow, a
search for understanding, for some
deeper meaning. Your writing left
behind to tell me more of your stories.
The beautiful sad-eyed dog grieving
against my leg. More time up on
Boston Hill cathartic, I am certain.
Soon, a trip out to Little Walnut.

Tender Revisions

Rudy was right about writing fueled by
grief. This most explosive outpouring.
New habits evolving. The simple act of
turning on the shower can unleash an
avalanche of words or just as likely tears.
A foray into town, while still anxious to
remain unseen. Fragile, unarmored.
No improvement to raw vulnerability.
Necessary embracing of new routines.
I claim your dining chair, your corner
of the sofa with revised pillows and
afghan so that the emptiness beside
me is somehow a little less obvious.
I yearn for more warmth. Five candles
lit. Straining to know Dylan's lyrics. New
images being printed and imprinted.

Easing into Past Tense

Nick comes up the steps weeping,
bereft that he had not read my text.
Sad for my sadness. He points out
that there are just five leaves
remaining on the pear tree. Early
harbinger of this dreaded fall. It
was then that I noticed the dog's
whining. Short whimpers from
his outpost on the gravel. I know.
You miss him, too. I've saved so much
of his voice. Readings. Online events.
Gifts from a poet and personal pearls
strung on my voicemail. Alternately
reviewing the images gathered on my
computer for the memorial. Still
unable to reassemble the magic.

Unmoored

Unmoored, floundering without the
perceived security you offered me.
Allowed, finally, to shed all that armor,
the carefully assembled persona of
the bold, strong single woman.
Even from the other room, you
always called out an inquiry to
be assured of my well-being
if you heard an unfamiliar sound.
When I giggled in response, you
happily joined the mirth, before
I could share its source.

You comfortably managed all our details,
so obvious in your displays of love.
I did not even know what utilities
provided for our serene shelter.
Travel became a new pleasure, as an
accessory to your long-legged
front row seat and early boarding ease,
always certain of each route, while
embracing the spell of an open road.
Upon entering the walled town of Arezzo
for the first time, you already knew
each turn and plaza to cross. Astounding
capacity in that navigator's mind.

Scattering Memories

I'll be back up here all too soon.
Come with me one last time?
Another wave of shock-like ice-
water reminds me that I am now
a solo sojourner, ready or not.
Gratitude ongoing for the container,
the beauty of this broad vista.

I cannot help but envision you
scaling that vertical end of the North
Pit, trailing determination as your
long golden legs found purchase.
Proving your dominance, cancer
and compression fractures be
damned. I was annoyed, channeling
my worried mother. The dog and I
retreating to low ground. And yes,
we went back up to the trail to
receive your triumphant grin.

Solitary Musings

Such deep sadness has taken root, deep in my belly. Hunger is now simply
a nuisance. The shining moments of optimism come erratically, leaving
me confounded that I may have perhaps dreamed them to be more banal
than true. The allure of the cloud cover of this season has lost its wonder,
as has the long-anticipated crop of white peaches. Will I ever find them
seductive again? I do muse about seduction sometimes, that too having
lost any yearning in these days of uncertainty and tears. I was practicing
believing in a safe and friendly world, as instructed. Hard to grasp, this
week. I struggle to dodge a state of panic, to trust that time is a construct,
and that we have an endless stream of it to create more worlds. I light
more lamps, and earlier, pondering some past embracing of fall, and
wondering if I could have found each day any more precious. The colors
and the red rock beckon. There is not yet an rsvp. Mornings seem better,
clearer, but today there was no work done. I go out into the evening,
attempting a slow waltz with the sunset sky offerings, certain that the dog
will comfort me, at least. The magnificence of the clouds does overwhelm
me, and I miss your nurturing presence in that appreciation. I return for
a second look, hoping not to stumble upon a carcass, a casualty of that
earlier window collision. After a disappointing cloud tour, I muster the will
to sit down with the leftover noodle bowl. Not at all as interesting as the
quintessential pepperoni and mushroom pizza of my vision, but effective
at quelling the gripping feeling for the moment. I consider a numbing glass
of wine but recognize the reality that it, too, will be deeply unsatisfying. As
my mild anticipation for a bit of brownie evaporates entirely, I'm reminded
of how my emotions tend to drain any appetite pretty completely. The
dog's entrance, to lean companionably on my shins, sharing the news of
the slightest sprinkling of rain, is far more useful in bolstering me. We both
miss your company, your laugh, your wonder and joy, so sharply, I can only
plead for respite before the dawning of any deeper truths.

Ornament Orange

From my nest of sorrow
I see only one
brilliant orange survivor.
A single leaf still on the pear tree
out the French door view.
Sighing return to
The Shape of a Hill,
I hunt for you in
your stories of your past.
The open page in my lap
reveals a line about
a box elder with
a single leaf
turned ornament orange.
Is that you,
reassuring me
that we can continue
to hear each other
through the veil?

My Own True North

Will the Indohyus return
from the sleep of extinction,
do you suppose?
The story resonating in its familiarity,
given current rising temperatures?
Perhaps my lesson in
more careful listening
to all that reverberates.
Not insisting on some
thunderous echolocation
to point my way.

And will you be back as well?
You temper this life now
in such a potent way.
Drawing my attention.
Tugging at my curiosity,
urging the reader and
the writer in me.

Some say fourteen years.
Prescription between lives.
So then must I find
my own version of
that flatbed truck,
to catch another cosmic ride
with your mysteries?
To feel seen in that
confounding way again?

It seems that first,
I must make peace with
the finality of this one.

Pondering the Wildness

Held in the firm grip of this surrounding wonder,
I yearn for more of the Gila's lessons.
First, the distinction between Wilderness and
National Forest. No less magnificent
or sacred in either case.
Oh. Contained *in* the Forest. I like that.
Within reach of the auspicious Continental Divide,
while snuggled at home in the lap of Boston Hill,
right where you left me,
I mourn my lack of retention...
And I need to know where I am,
as well as whom, in this new
and ill-fitting costume.

Snub-nosed Cooke's Peak was easy,
and I've got the Floor-EEE-duhs down.
The Burros, uncertain.
And isn't that Tres Something over there?
Sometimes gazing at a distant Arizona
or into the mouth of Mexico.
Easy to envision Geronimo
strategizing at that height.
The word-hustler in me
gulps this new language:
Mogollon. Mescalero.
And Vanadium sounds surely of value.

Scouting diligently for sources of gratitude
these days, Gaia graciously complies.
The fox, poised for prey, on the
way to the cliff dwellings.
The birds, too, no doubt offer me tutelage.
Gambel's quail dialogue lures me,
whether for assembly or alarm.
The precious revelation that the dog hears me
in the silence. And that I must just listen
harder for his replies, and now for yours.

Celebrating You

Pouring hot water into my mug first,
the way you would have, I'm reminded of
how I am filled up with you. Your determination.
Great gulps of your wisdom. Hopefully your
kindness. So much of your essence.
I pick up my tear-spattered glasses,
reminder of the bottomless
reservoir of my grief.

I'm asked, Was it good, this celebration of
your diverse and significant life?
Comforting? Uplifting? Or hard.
So *very* hard without your strength
carrying me. And yes, to all of that.
Everyone showed up in their truth
and with their love, to launch your
last book and to hold me up.
Such a staggering outpouring of creativity.
Tom and Jade, and Dogstar colored the room
with their joyful sounds and presence.

Jesse and Sylvia had a tree planted
for you in a national forest,
causing me to weep for the beauty
of such a perfect gesture.
I yearn to know that special tree,
and then remember that
you are everywhere now.
Vowing still to go out there
more often, to speak to you.

I came home wearing your black dress hat.
Big brim. Blocked hard.
The going-out one.
While donned in practicality,
driving into that setting winter sun
blazing into my eyes,
it did feel oddly empowering,
and comforting, too.
Conflicting resistance to
returning to a home without you,
competing with the requirement
of being there in the quietude
of my sorrow.

In last night's dream, Daddy walked
quietly beside me for a little distance.
Distracted by life,
I didn't appreciate that comfort
until the fork in the road
where he left me.
An affirmation, I think, of how
I treasured my time with you each day,
and that despite the lists,
the necessities of this life,
I will just be in the stillness
with you today.
All love.

Sowing Seeds in a New Way

Unruly emotions, often interrupting
each other to vie for my attention.
I recognize the internal flashing yellow light
that warns of my impending slide
towards the abyss and with alarming velocity.
Scavenging among my scattered thoughts
for alternative brands of salvation,
practicing focus on this one immediate
shining day. Vowing the gratitude practice,
beginning with the lavishly blossoming
peach tree, resplendent in early Spring pink.
More planting sounds appealing,
though historically an expensive endeavor
without many triumphs.
There are all those seeds to try, yet again.
Consistent watering, always the test.
Currently, regenerating kitchen scraps.
The red cabbage, exploring the interior
of the refrigerator drawer, reminded me
that it was past time to begin. Can we
do that, too? Fiercely grab this opportunity
to reimagine humanity.
A chance for so much creativity,
and in a slower, kinder, healthier world.

New Growth, Regardless

Honey, there are violets in the park!
And it's not quite February yet.
You know. The little park down on Market.
I hope my memory doesn't worsen,
as this new life barges ahead,
dragging the unwilling through
the tatters of the precious past.
You worked so hard to get me oriented.
To teach me the language of all those mountains,
and what direction, each crooked street.
Too intent on each alchemical moment,
you must have thought me a terrible student,
endlessly distracted by all the new and shiny things.

Did you suspect? I have to ask.
So abrupt. That surreal month of hospice
notwithstanding. Deep in logistics,
legalities, and pain management,
I still marveled at those twinkling eyes
exuding love and gratitude,
when I held your water glass to your parched lips.
So many questions I might have asked
had I not been in such a place of shock.
You continued to drive our bus even then.
Destination: stubborn determination.
In my mind now, without that looming specter,
I imagine weaving miracles into dreams and ventures,
drawing castles and gondolas on your wrist.

They keep asking if I sense your presence now,
those who know such things.
Maybe it's true that I'm not ready yet,
or that you still have much work to do, there.
This, the ultimate initiation.
But I've begun to feel your arms
around me when even the glorious
morning sun brings sad weeping.
I need so much to hear your voice.

I Need to Say This

Some mental gymnastics,
a trick of the mind, I've
heard some speculation.
That you are simply walking
down another street.
Or beyond a fork in the path.
I often catch myself watching
for you to come out of the trees,
come down off the hill
towards me. I try to imagine
a future. Me, in this life.
New rituals, they suggest.
How about a tradition of
a music jam on this hill
every year on your birthday?
Invite everyone who missed your
launch. Get Tom and Jade to come.
Fill me up with joyful sounds.

It is true that since you left
(some days, I can't help but see it
that way), I cannot imagine anything
else good happening in this life.
I spend some time wondering.
A lot of time, actually.
Is this some karmic lesson in
selflessness? Some balance
for the selfish only child?

Daddy died at sixty-nine, too.
Mother had nineteen more years
spent mostly alone in that house.
I carry the shame of not paying
enough attention. How can I not
speculate on my murky
vision of who to be and
what to accomplish now?

Types of Resistance

I think that today's tally is a positive one.
But then I haven't left the house yet.
Albertson's feels like a manageable goal.
That's assuming the bathing and dressing
are surmounted successfully.
Meditation would have been so valuable.
The lure that I often connect
with my love there.
But I couldn't stop crying,
surrendered, and returned home.
I have to trust that a brief interlude was
catharsis of some kind.

This afternoon, a walk on Boston Hill.
I envision more and more foot traffic there.
Lonely, separated beings trudging
the trails with prescribed distance between.
So many new practices in Covid time.
The dogs deliriously circling between us,
relieved to be released from angst-filled homes.
We remain the required six feet apart.
Yet didn't I read that a viral sneeze travels ten feet?
Later, I will go to Elise's garden to select starts.
Surely that will contribute. Planting, life-affirming.
Dinner sounds difficult. I do remain endlessly
grateful for the gift of this isolated village.

I watch the waves of creativity
swirling around my paralysis.
Denise so aptly described the bunker of
solitude, knowing it so intimately.
Others meet to exchange poems.
Outdoors, of course.
A flurry of suggested online offerings.
Yoga, music, drawing class. All seem
possible and certainly beneficial. But a
virtual exchange of poems?
Tributes to my love. Without him here
to comfort me. I don't know where I can find
that kind of courage right now.

Tunes Through the Veil

We settle into our new selves,
some more in search of new personas,
as opposed to this unmoored limbo
between worlds, shrouded vision ahead.
And now masked in a more literal way.
I loved the one with the big block letters
that said VOTE. But I couldn't find it again.

The most accessible version of myself
wears a sun hat, hiking boots, breathable
clothing, even as I still can't get my breath.
My pack with special canine water bottle
and hiking poles to grasp my way up this
mountain. Trying not to think of Sisyphus.
Selecting uncertainty over futility.

Writing in my head, as the dog canters
looping circles around me, reappearing
periodically. Just often enough to prove
ongoing guardianship. We each look for
breaks in the precious patches of shade.
The fleeting sacrament of morning breezes
wakes my senses, affirms this beauty.
I vow, meanwhile, to accomplish this
ascent earlier, or instead to commune
with more trees. I will acquire sunscreen.

I find myself cleaning out the neglected corners.
Attending to random projects to bring fresh air,
space, motion to my inertia. Pulling out the
abandoned bicycle for refurbishing. Beginning
yet another thrift store box. And in my rummaging,
I stumble upon the poem you offered to our
meeting. Full of reverence, anticipation,
and truths you had yet to share. So oddly
comforting now. And then the harmonicas that
I knew had a place in your past. Not just a
couple, but ten, total. That's how I knew
that they were yours.

Recording the Unspoken

Upon finding themselves in love,
some will write what they cannot yet
say aloud. The magnitude overwhelming,
bringing reverence, triggering old fears.

Upon finding that poem of examination
of new feelings for me, these years later
and now so starkly alone,
a dose of wonder is required.
Both for the significance imparted,
collectively known, in that moment,
and for the puzzle that I was in such
deep immersion, not to have
written passionately, myself.

Notes addressed to my beloved,
in my customary forthright way.
Now mementos of that whirlwind time.
Truly a sense of falling.
Tumbling willingly towards
some irrevocable depth of being.
I made absolutely no attempt
to retain contact with the ground,
to find any armor to shield me.

I could sense those efforts happening
on behalf of us both.
I have to wonder now, too,
if I have gathered such fears
in the intervening years.
If I would stride deliberately
toward another possibility
for such sacred wonder.

Palm Reading

I cannot help but think first of
Fauci's face palm, subtle as it was.
Seeming attempt to squelch laughter at
the absurdity of the Cirque that
this has become. Lunacy, greed,
subterfuge run rampant.
Rampant, the descriptor for our
times. The endless and futile quest
to accurately narrate this
twilight zone. Would it offer ablution,
I wonder, to just put down all those
marvelous adjectives on a page,
for posterity? Like the cleansing, purging
aspect of writing the morning pages?

And the determination of my planting.
Knowing the inevitable companion lessons.
Visualizing the curative flow with vigilant watering.
This year, herbs and vegetables. Searching
for some measure of sovereignty?

I keep plodding up my rocky hill,
certain of the healing value in ascent.
Necessity for both dog and me.
Reveling each time in the rewarding vistas,
grace in such a remote and reflective place.
This week, in an offering to serenity, or closure,
or acceptance, I guess, I took some ashes to scatter
from the precipice of that rock face you so
triumphantly scaled. My own cathartic triumph,
my palm infused with yours.

Incomplete

Both of us restless today, the dog
and I. An attempted outing to the Buzz
to see if a poem arose. The way that you
would have. But the clever canine water
bottle oozed into my handbag, drenching
my writing journal along with the copy of
your death certificate carried just in case.
Curious, to see this physical evidence at
a time when you already fill and refill my mind.
Such an abundance of writing held in limbo.
Captured moments never edited or entered
for some unimagined future. I fan the damp pages
in the sun, wondering if this ongoing stream
of emotion can be absorbed in some kindred way.
I envision driving with the curious dog, destination
some far horizon. Also, your way. Reality, however,
describes a slow shuffle about the now diminished
kingdom, baby steps in projects concluded,
tools put away; dead plants removed
with reverent apology.

There are longing looks into the bedroom,
from the dog now stationed close beside me.
Random wandering into rooms unexplored
before now. Is he sharing this phase of
loneliness and yearning? Only a phase, right?
Not a long slow slide toward the abyss, as I fear.
I grapple with the temptation for anger
for a life aborted, with so much more to do.
And then there are the tears at most any
provocation. The questions jostle right behind.
No resolution emerging. Just those shining
moments of peace, surrendering to the unanswered.

Left Behind

I study the treasured letter in my hand
after my mother's passing. Penned on the
envelope in her writing is the directive,
'Keep forever!' It's from her dear friend
of sixty-some years, written just to be
certain that she knows how much she is
loved, her wisdom and friendship highly
valued for so long. What a precious gift.
I replace the letter tenderly in the
keepsake box, musing over what merits
curating. After I am gone from this world,
will someone open that envelope, curious
about its place in forever? They likely won't
have known her. And certainly not her friend,
Patricia. Sobering, to be at the tail end of
this lineage, keeper of the legacy.

And now, I roam the crooked cottage, examining
things with that same tenderness. Pondering
what should have meaning, right here where
you left everything. That silver bud vase honoring
your mother. Complete with its faded
silk irises, ode to her beloved garden club.
Shall I hold it dear as you did? I yearn to know
where the little painted rocking horse hails from.
And that quirky brass mouse. It always makes me
smile. What is that worth? The African figure has
traveled to the thrift box and back, uncertain.

No doubt from your time teaching African
drumming in Taos. But in truth, I don't know the stories.
There was never enough time. Like you always said,
I'm making this up. Just as I culled the family treasures,
I suppose that over time, we must keep choosing
what to leave behind, a vignette for posterity.

My mind travels to the California tribe that I
left there. Since shattered and scattered across
so many states. Every year or so, my friend and I
write a vow to speak again, sharing our deep
connection. Not once since leaving have we
manifested that intention. Then I think of a
dear long-time friend now in Manhattan, with
both of us traversing so many life changes.
We once always phoned in our birthday month.
But then life grew too large, too demanding.
Now, in pandemic times, we all hesitate to plan
any reunion, considering the very literal possibility
that we might each die alone, with all our
things strewn exactly where we left them.

My traveling mind considers the abruptness
of the departures surrounding me. Both
parents, whose hearts no longer sustained,
unanticipated and deeply shocking.

My great love, whose cancer suddenly
announced the upper hand, giving us
barely time to cope, to marry, to consider
how to die with grace and any peace.
Most recently, my friend's husband, who
I did not get to know well enough, left
suddenly, too. The heart, yet again. The
conclusion is the heart, it seems. Keeper
of all that matters to those of us left behind.

Elevation Makes Me Cry

Prophets and poets would populate the
mountaintops, I imagined. And I suppose
some rogue explorer, bolder and more
agile than I at this stage of the venture.
But the highest peak, the hardest work,
the doctoral course, I insist, was the ultimate
triathlon of tangled emotions and endless
exhaustion of losing my love, my heart
husband, and way too soon. The anniversary
of your taking flight turned out to be a
wonder. Bewildering and remedial jolt,
reviewing the assaulting emotions, the
constricted chest, the inability for much
exertion. Gratitude for the dog's insistence
on climbing our neighboring elevation,
though on some days impossibly high.

And now, a new sierra. This time of my
selection. Empowering, right? Emerging
rather abruptly from that deep well of
desolation, the way suddenly undeniable,
brightly illuminated and energizing. I
scatter gratitude for this growth opportunity.
Undaunted by the obvious learning curve,
the growing list of consultants and courses.
The fact that you already owned so many
of those skills when you began all those
years ago. So many circles this work will
complete. A spiral course to new heights.

Another Fool's Journey

Last week, circling the drain. Sliding
for the abyss as described. My grief
renewed, more robust than ever with
that weight on my chest, the eternal
well of ready tears, always so tender.
Never linear, never succumbing to
rules or patterns. This time, perhaps
simply one last imposing roadblock to the
reassembly of my being. Vital to the
required forward motion for the
balance of this labyrinthine odyssey.

Reminded of my unalome with its
circuitous path, this last grave detour
so plainly portrayed. I am left to ponder
recognition of any proximity to totality,
should that occur. Visually, it would
appear that this juncture represents a
significant milestone, leading now to
the final straightaway, the expanding
light of knowing. Of new truths in this
climb to awareness. And now, a vehicle
in repose, in my lap all this time. Shift
occurring without prompt. My delight
over this realization energizes and
empowers me as I stretch my wings,
newly confident in my competence and
in your guidance for such flight feathers.

Incarnation Incomplete

I will know you by your laugh, I am
certain, and by mine that you provoke.
Surely that will be our cue. At least one
sacred thread. Okay, that kiss will tell.
No doubt for that holy exchange.
Just trust that I will know. Deep within
my being. Whoever that being may be.
It is said that sometimes we switch
genders. Would we opt for that path?
What lessons on our next list? Those
trials not yet borne. And in a world
unimagined. Could we choose ourselves
as poets again? Must I simply accept
that you may have been complete in
this journey, as I apparently was not?

Assimilation, as Promised

Somehow, unknowingly, I had slipped through the veil,
gravitating instinctively to your side, searching out
that glowing smile. I had wondered how you could
smile that way, as you lay dying. And now, you showed
serene joy but no surprise at my appearance, continuing to
finalize your new acquisition, a long heavy woven neck
chain of a silver tone. A sort of snake-like cable with
an intricate pattern. Perhaps platinum to justify its
precious nature. You commented that you could
now do such extravagant things, without earthly
expenses. We were in a very upscale and elegant
jewelry shop, it seemed. No place you would ever
have frequented in this life. I stopped myself from
verbalizing my experience, that it was too long
for you, and no doubt billed by the inch. Inevitable
to get caught on things, at least the things of this realm.
But it nestled beautifully against your tanned chest,
inside the shirt that I did not recognize: delicate cotton
voile, in a plaid of soft, dreamy colors. Totally unlike
anything you might have ever selected. Feeling
your smiling forward motion, directing me out
the door, I moved on ahead into a narrow cobbled
street, European in feeling. As I turned back,
waiting for you to follow me out as I expected,
and curious over your delay, I glanced down at myself,
slowly grasping that I was seeing your chest,
the chain, the lovely shirt, realizing that you truly were
now a part of me, nestled perfectly in my heart.

The author with the magical Heka dog

Stewart and Pamela celebrating Italy

Biography

Pamela Warren Williams is a poet and artist, with a fine art and design background, and a lifelong habit of artistic expression. Her heartland upbringing provided the springboard for thirty expansive years in the San Francxisco area, where the vibrant culture, spectacular geography, and her antique/collectible business offered a parade of provocative fodder for her voice. New Mexico's extreme contrasts and rich history are now fueling alchemical inspiration and empowerment through its proffered seductions and mysterious remnants of multi-cultural heritage, feeding her current writing and assemblage work and her rebirthing of her late husband's publishing business. She searches out poignant truths provoked by the heartbreaking beauty of a miniature wing on her studio floor, or the current pain on our border, and follows the ties that either bind or tear us apart. Her poems and assemblages have appeared in the *Poets Speak: Walls* and *Survival* anthologies, four Lummox anthologies, *Live Out Loud, We Don't Break* anthology, *Poetry Lovers and Writing in a Woman's Voice* epubs, ElPalacio.org, and her own collection, *Hair On Fire* (Mercury Heartlink). Her writing is most recently driven by the loss of her husband, inspiring diving more deeply into the miracles and grace of this journey

Made in the USA
Middletown, DE
11 April 2021

37387242R10068